PARASAUROLOPHUS

by Janet Riehecky
illustrated by Andre LeBlanc

THE CHILD'S WORLD

MANKATO, MN

*Grateful appreciation is expressed to
Bret S. Beall, Research Consultant,
Field Museum of Natural History, Chicago,
Illinois, who reviewed this book to
insure its accuracy.*

Library of Congress Cataloging in Publication Data

Riehecky, Janet, 1953-
   Parasaurolophus / by Janet Riehecky ; illustrated by Andre
LeBlanc.
      p. cm. — (Dinosaur books)
   Summary: Describes the physical characteristics and probable
behavior of this duck-billed dinosaur.
   ISBN 0-89565-633-7
   1. Parasaurolophus—Juvenile literature.   [1. Parasaurolophus.
2. Dinosaurs.]   I. LeBlanc, Andre, ill.   II. Title.   III. Series:
Riehecky, Janet, 1953-   Dinosaur books.
QE862.O65R536   1990
567.9'7—dc20   90-42518
                                                            CIP
                                                            AC

PARASAUROLOPHUS

Once, huge dinosaurs wandered the earth. They left behind skeletons, eggs, and footprints. These help us imagine what the world of the dinosaurs looked like.

But we really don't have much of an idea
what it sounded like.

Did a dinosaur's tail CRACK like a whip
as it fought off an attacker?

Would a dinosaur roar a challenge when
it wanted to fight?

Were there some dinosaurs that hummed
a song to attract a mate?

And were there others that barked out a
warning when danger was near?

We can be pretty sure that the world of the dinosaurs echoed with the thud of gigantic feet, the splash of water, and the buzz of insects. But we have no idea what, if any, sounds the dinosaurs themselves made. There may have been barks and howls, grunts and growls of all different sorts. Scientists think it is likely that many of the dinosaurs could make sounds, but they don't know what kinds. They can, however, make a good guess at the sound made by one dinosaur.

Scientists think that one type of dinosaur may have "played a horn." That dinosaur was the Parasaurolophus (par-uh-sawr-OL-uh-fus). Scientists think it could blow air through the long, hollow crest on its head to make a noise like a horn's.

The crest of the Parasaurolophus was a very long, thin tube of bone. It began at the dinosaur's nose and stretched up way above its head. On some Parasaurolophus, the crest reached six feet long—that meant the crest alone was longer than many people! Scientists have found some Parasaurolophus with smaller crests. They think these were either females or young Parasaurolophus.

The Parasaurolophus' crest was hollow inside. A tube for air went up from each nostril to the tip of the crest and then curved back down like a trombone. All the air a Parasaurolophus breathed had to make this long journey. Not even Pinocchio had a nose that long!

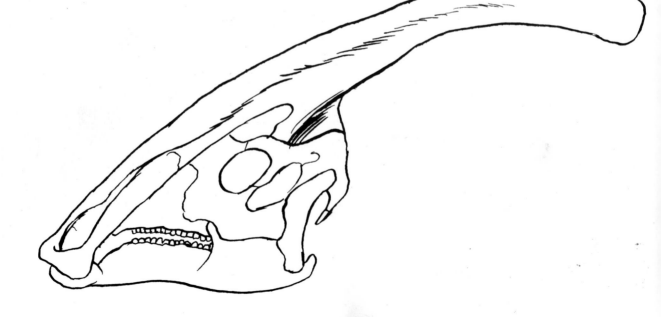

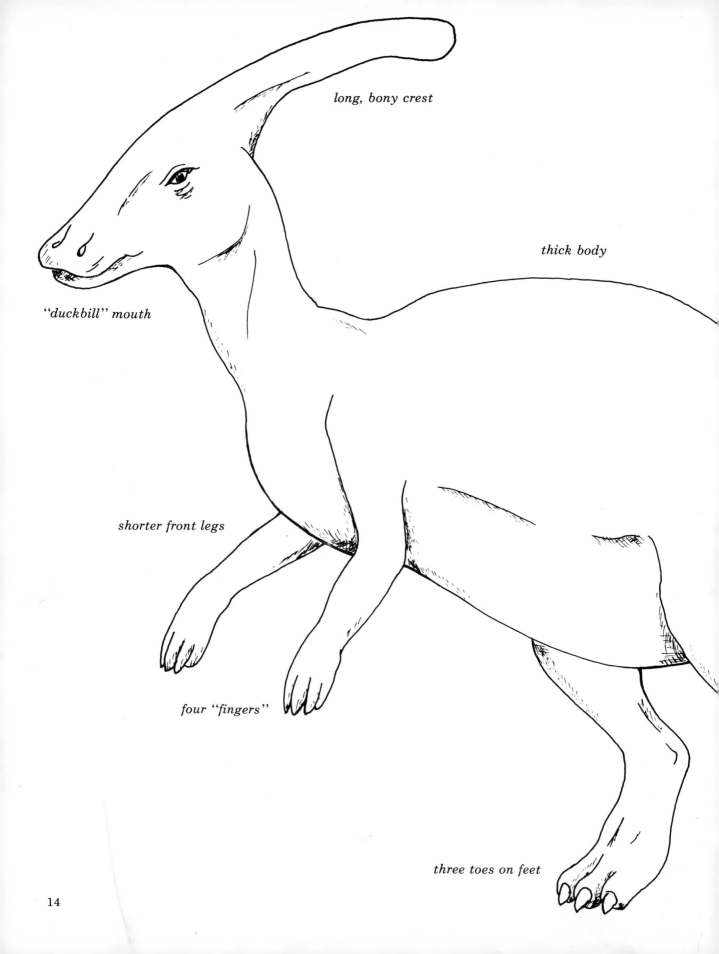

long, bony crest

thick body

"duckbill" mouth

shorter front legs

four "fingers"

three toes on feet

Scientists wondered for many years why the Parasaurolophus had this large, unusual crest. In every other way, it was a pretty ordinary dinosaur. It was a plant eater of a kind nicknamed "duckbilled" because its mouth was long and flat like a duck's bill. It stood on two strong back legs, with shorter front legs that it could use as arms. It was about thirty feet long and sixteen feet tall. It probably weighed three or four tons. This was about the size of a bus—or an average dinosaur.

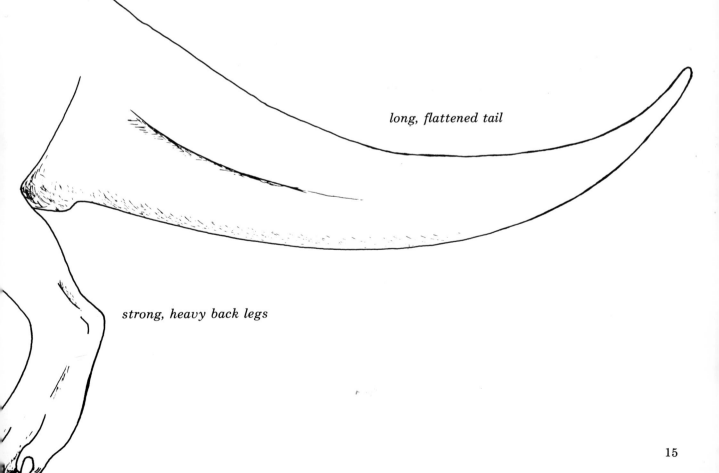

long, flattened tail

strong, heavy back legs

In studying the unusual crest of the Parasaurolophus, one scientist noticed that the crest was shaped something like a horn. He made a model of the crest and blew air through it. It made a low, musical tone. Many scientists believe the Parasaurolophus blew air out through its crest making a sound which could be heard miles away.

The Parasaurolophus could have used different tones to communicate different messages. It might have called to members of its herd or sounded an alarm if danger approached. Imagine how a forest might have echoed with the sound of a whole herd of those gigantic beasts honking at a Tyrannosaurus to go away!

Making sounds might not have been the only use the Parasaurolophus found for its crest. Scientists have suggested all sorts of other uses.

One of the first ideas they suggested was that the crest was used as a snorkel. They pictured the Parasaurolophus swimming underwater with just its crest stuck out for it to breathe through. There was a small problem with this idea, though. The scientists couldn't find a hole in the tip of the crest. If no air could get into the crest, how could the Parasaurolophus have breathed through it? It would have been like trying to drink through a straw with one end blocked. So, the scientists decided that wasn't such a good idea.

Some scientists thought the Parasaurolophus might have stored air in the crest to use while underwater. But only a small amount of air could be kept in the crest. It wouldn't have helped the dinosaur stay under for very long. So the crest probably wasn't used for that either.

Scientists today have many other, better ideas. Some think the crest was used to push branches aside as the Parasaurolophus made its way through thick forests. The cassowary, a large, flightless, Australian bird, uses its crest for that today. Another idea is that the crest brought cool air close to the Parasaurolophus' brain to keep it from getting too hot.

Many scientists believe that when a Parasaurolophus wanted to attract a mate, it showed off with its crest. The Parasaurolophus might also have raised its crest as a warning to another dinosaur to go away.

The crest could also have helped the Parasaurolophus smell things. Since the Parasaurolophus had no real defense against meat-eating dinosaurs, it needed some way to tell if a meat eater was sneaking up. With that big nose, it could smell the meat eater while there was still plenty of time to run.

Scientists don't know for sure if the Parasaurolophus used its crest in any of these ways. They continue to look for clues and ideas.

Scientists have found other clues which make them think that Parasaurolophus lived in herds. They believe large herds lived on the coastal plains near swamps and rivers. Parasaurolophus probably liked both land and water. They appear to have been both good runners and good swimmers. Their long, flattened tails balanced them as they ran or helped them glide through the water. Some scientists even think they had webbed fingers, which helped them push themselves through the water.

Water was probably a good escape route for a Parasaurolophus when it was being chased by a meat eater. When it came time to eat, though, the Parasaurolophus chose dry land. Its strong jaws were made for eating tough plants, such as pine needles, leaves, and different fruits and seeds.

The Parasaurolophus' cheeks were loaded with good grinding teeth. And if any of the teeth broke or wore out, new ones came right in. In fact, a Parasaurolophus may have grown more than ten thousand teeth during its lifetime.

Scientists have not found any Parasaurolophus eggs or babies, but they do think the Parasaurolophus took care of its young. Other duckbilled dinosaurs raised their babies in carefully guarded nurseries. They fed and watched over them until they were big enough to take care of themselves. It seems likely that the Parasaurolophus behaved as other duckbilled dinosaurs did.

Certainly the Parasaurolophus knew how to survive. They lived right up to the end of the age of dinosaurs, outliving all other duckbilled dinosaurs. But sixty-five million years ago, the last dinosaurs on earth died, including the Parasaurolophus.

Never again will the world echo with the sound of those gigantic feet or the sound of a Parasaurolophus calling to its friends.

Dinosaur Fun

In the world today animals make many different and fascinating sounds: the howl of a coyote, the song of a humpback whale, the roar of a lion. Dinosaurs may have made just as many different kinds of sounds. Imagine what kinds of sounds big dinosaurs, such as Apatosaurus, Diplodocus, or Triceratops might have made. How might little dinosaurs, such as Compsognathus or Coelophysis have sounded? And would Tyrannosaurus have made the loudest noise of all? You can find out ways animals use sound by reading books such as *Animal Communication* by Janet McDonnell. Then make up your own dinosaur noises for your favorite dinosaurs and record them on a tape recorder.